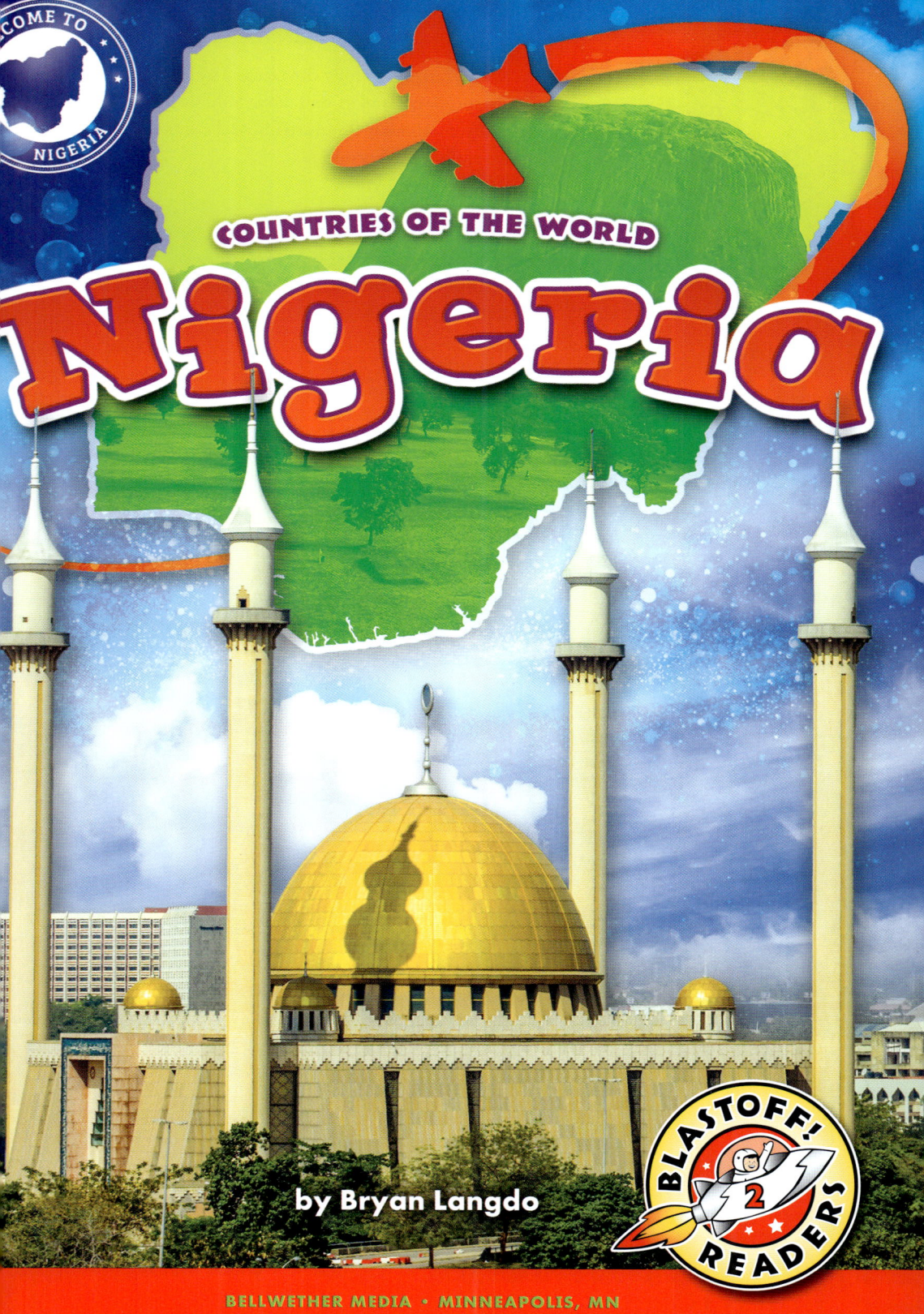

COUNTRIES OF THE WORLD

Nigeria

by Bryan Langdo

BELLWETHER MEDIA • MINNEAPOLIS, MN

Blastoff! Readers are carefully developed by literacy experts to build reading stamina and move students toward fluency by combining standards-based content with developmentally appropriate text.

Level 1 provides the most support through repetition of high-frequency words, light text, predictable sentence patterns, and strong visual support.

Level 2 offers early readers a bit more challenge through varied sentences, increased text load, and text-supportive special features.

Level 3 advances early-fluent readers toward fluency through increased text load, less reliance on photos, advancing concepts, longer sentences, and more complex special features.

★ **Blastoff! Universe**

Reading Level

Grade K

Grades 1–3

Grade 4

This edition first published in 2025 by Bellwether Media, Inc.

No part of this publication may be reproduced in whole or in part without written permission of the publisher. For information regarding permission, write to Bellwether Media, Inc., Attention: Permissions Department, 6012 Blue Circle Drive, Minnetonka, MN 55343.

Library of Congress Cataloging-in-Publication Data

Names: Langdo, Bryan, author.
Title: Nigeria / by Bryan Langdo.
Other titles: Blastoff! readers. 2, Countries of the world.
Description: Minneapolis, MN : Bellwether Media, Inc., 2025. | Series: Blastoff! readers. Countries of the world | Includes bibliographical references and index. | Audience: Ages 5-8 | Audience: Grades 2-3 | Summary: "Relevant images match informative text in this introduction to Nigeria. Intended for students in kindergarten through third grade" – Provided by publisher.
Identifiers: LCCN 2024039308 (print) | LCCN 2024039309 (ebook) | ISBN 9798893042313 (library binding) | ISBN 9798893043280 (ebook)
Subjects: LCSH: Nigeria–Juvenile literature.
Classification: LCC DT515.22 .L36 2025 (print) | LCC DT515.22 (ebook) | DDC 966.9–dc23/eng/20240826
LC record available at https://lccn.loc.gov/2024039308
LC ebook record available at https://lccn.loc.gov/2024039309

Text copyright © 2025 by Bellwether Media, Inc. BLASTOFF! READERS and associated logos are trademarks and/or registered trademarks of Bellwether Media, Inc.

Editor: Suzane Nguyen   Designer: Laura Sowers

Printed in the United States of America, North Mankato, MN.

Table of Contents

All About Nigeria	4
Land and Animals	6
Life in Nigeria	12
Nigeria Facts	20
Glossary	22
To Learn More	23
Index	24

All About Nigeria

Abuja

Nigeria is a large country in western Africa. Its capital is Abuja.

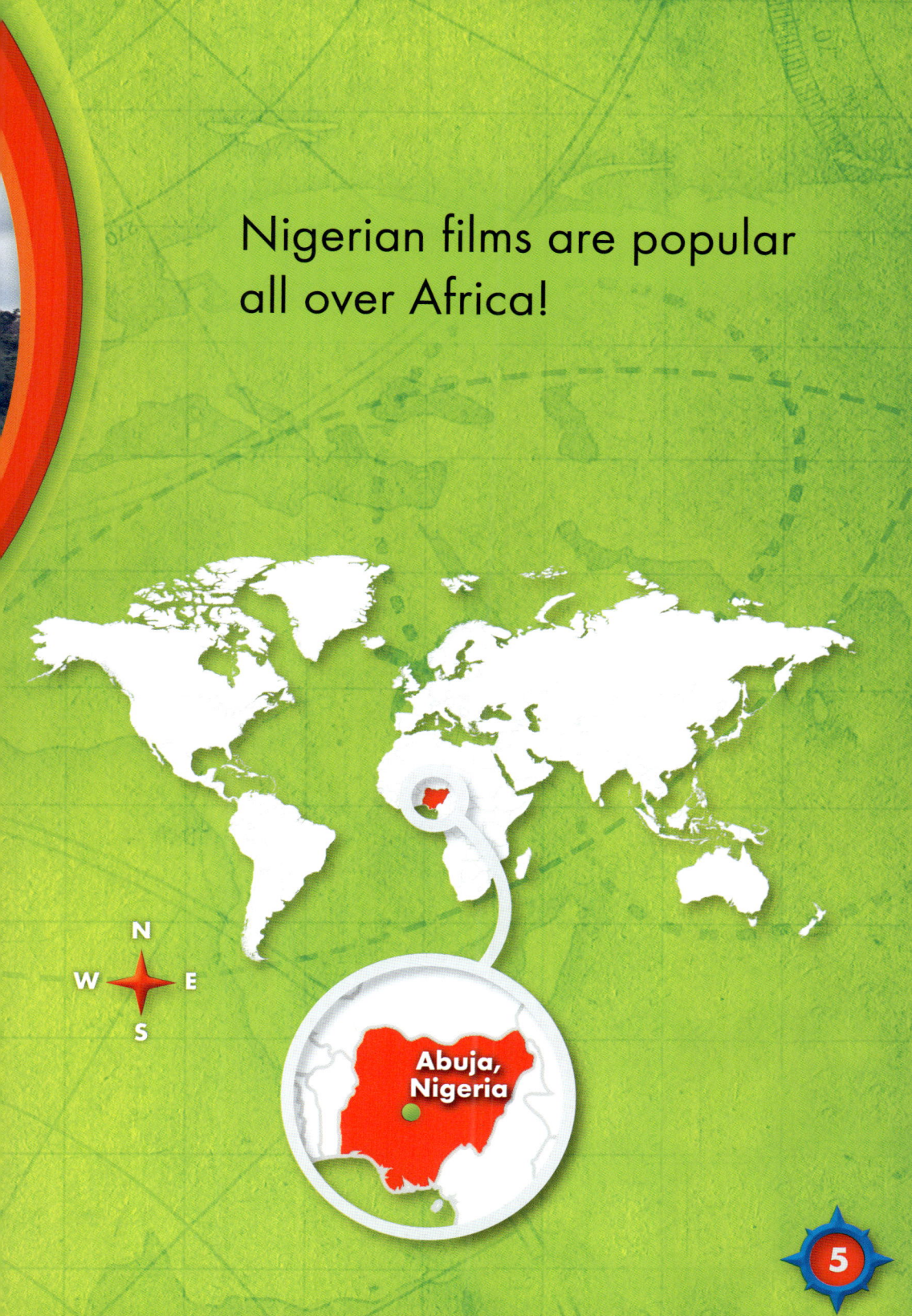

Nigerian films are popular all over Africa!

Abuja, Nigeria

Land and Animals

Plains span most of Nigeria. **Plateaus** rise in the middle.

Rain forests cover the southwest. Swamps line the coast. The Niger River drains into the sea.

rain forest

Niger River

Length: 2,600 miles (4,184 kilometers)
Famous For: the longest river in West Africa

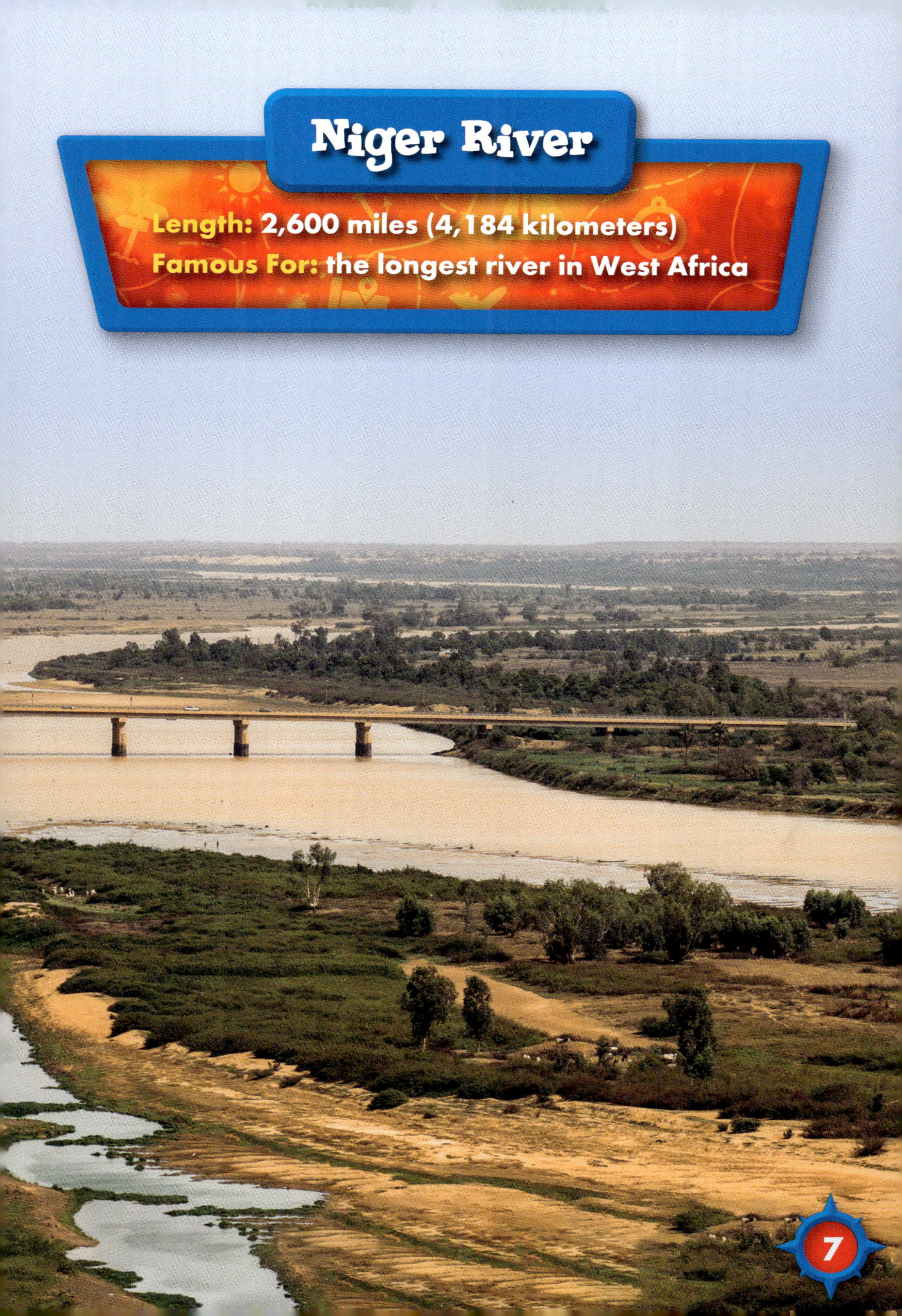

dry season

Nigeria is a **tropical** country. It has a rainy season and a dry season.

The north has warmer weather. More rain falls in the south.

rainy season

Most of Nigeria's wildlife live in **national parks**. Elephants eat fruit from trees. Puff adders hunt for meals.

African forest elephant

Animals of Nigeria

African forest elephant

puff adder

African fish eagle

hippopotamus

African fish eagles dive for fish. Hippopotamuses swim in rivers.

Life in Nigeria

Nigeria is the most **populated** country in Africa. It is home to over 250 **ethnic** groups.

People mainly speak English, but over 500 **native** languages are spoken, too!

Music plays a big part in Nigerian **culture**. The country's film **industry** is called Nollywood.

Soccer is a favorite sport. Basketball and boxing are also popular.

basketball

Jollof rice is a popular dish. The rice is cooked in tomato sauce. *Iyan* is pounded yams.

Nigerian Foods

jollof rice

iyan

efo riro

suya

pounding yams

Efo riro is a vegetable stew. *Suya* is spicy, grilled meat!

Calabar Carnival

October 1 is Independence Day. People wear green and white to parades.

Every December is the Calabar Carnival. Nigerians dance in costumes at street parties!

Nigeria Facts

Size:
356,669 square miles
(923,768 square kilometers)

Population:
236,747,130 (2024)

National Holiday:
Independence Day (October 1)

Main Languages:
English, over 500 native languages

Capital City:
Abuja

Famous Face

Name: Yemisi Ogunleye

Famous For: Olympic gold medalist in shot put

Religions

- Christian: 46%
- other: 0.5%
- Muslim: 53.5%

Top Landmarks

Abuja National Mosque

Freedom Park

Olumo Rock

Glossary

culture—the beliefs, arts, and ways of life in a place or society

ethnic—related to races or large groups of people who share things such as customs, religion, and language

industry—businesses that provide a certain product or service

national parks—areas of land that a country sets aside for natural or historic reasons

native—related to something that is originally from a certain place

plains—areas of flat land with few trees

plateaus—flat, raised areas of land

populated—having people living in a place

rain forests—thick, green forests that receive a lot of rain

tropical—related to a warm place near the equator

To Learn More

AT THE LIBRARY

Klepeis, Alicia Z., and Donna Reynolds. *Nigeria*. Buffalo, N.Y.: Cavendish Square Publishing, 2023.

Spanier, Kristine. *Nigeria*. Minneapolis, Minn.: Jump!, 2020.

Ventura, Marne. *Foods from Nigeria*. Parker, Colo.: The Child's World, 2024.

ON THE WEB

FACTSURFER

Factsurfer.com gives you a safe, fun way to find more information.

1. Go to www.factsurfer.com.
2. Enter "Nigeria" into the search box and click 🔍.
3. Select your book cover to see a list of related content.

Index

Abuja, 4, 5
Africa, 4, 5, 12
animals, 10, 11
basketball, 15
boxing, 15
Calabar Carnival, 18, 19
capital (see Abuja)
coast, 6
culture, 14
dry season, 8
English 12
films, 5, 14
food, 16, 17
Independence Day, 18
map, 5
music, 14
national parks, 10
native languages, 12
Niger River, 6, 7

Nigeria facts, 20-21
people, 12, 18, 19
plains, 6
plateaus, 6
rain forests, 6
rainy season, 8, 9
say hello, 13
soccer, 15
swamps, 6

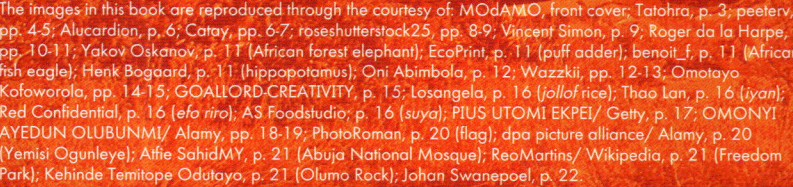

The images in this book are reproduced through the courtesy of: MOdAMO, front cover; Tatohra, p. 3; peetery, pp. 4-5; Alucardion, p. 6; Catay, pp. 6-7; roseshutterstock25, pp. 8-9; Vincent Simon, p. 9; Roger da la Harpe, pp. 10-11; Yakov Oskanov, p. 11 (African forest elephant); EcoPrint, p. 11 (puff adder); benoit_f, p. 11 (African fish eagle); Henk Bogaard, p. 11 (hippopotamus); Oni Abimbola, p. 12; Wazzkii, pp. 12-13; Omotayo Kofoworola, pp. 14-15; GOALLORD-CREATIVITY, p. 15; Losangela, p. 16 (*jollof* rice); Thao Lan, p. 16 (*iyan*); Red Confidential, p. 16 (*efo riro*); AS Foodstudio, p. 16 (*suya*); PIUS UTOMI EKPEI/ Getty, p. 17; OMONYI AYEDUN OLUBUNMI/ Alamy, pp. 18-19; PhotoRoman, p. 20 (flag); dpa picture alliance/ Alamy, p. 20 (Yemisi Ogunleye); Affie SahidMY, p. 21 (Abuja National Mosque); ReoMartins/ Wikipedia, p. 21 (Freedom Park); Kehinde Temitope Odutayo, p. 21 (Olumo Rock); Johan Swanepoel, p. 22.